AMERICA HAS

FUN

The Roaring Twenties

Sean Price

Raintree

Chicago, Illinois

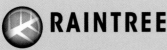

RAINTREE

TO ORDER:
☎ Phone Customer Service **888-454-2279**
💻 Visit **www.heinemannraintree.com** to browse our catalog and order online.

©2009 Raintree
a division of Pearson Education Limited
Chicago, Illinois

Editorial: Adam Miller
Design: Ryan Frieson, Kimberly R. Miracle, and Betsy Wernert
Photo Research: Tracy Cummins
Production: Victoria Fitzgerald

Originated by DOT Gradations Ltd
Printed and bound by Leo Paper Group

ISBN-13: 978-1-4109-3111-5 (hc)
ISBN-10: 1-4109-3111-0 (hc)
ISBN-13: 978-1-4109-3120-7 (pb)
ISBN-10: 1-4109-3120-X (pb)

13 12 11 10 09
10 9 8 7 6 5 4 3 2 1

Library of Congress Cataloging-in-Publication Data
Price, Sean.
   America has fun : the Roaring Twenties / Sean Price.
      p. cm. -- (American history through primary sources)
   Includes bibliographical references and index.
   ISBN 978-1-4109-3111-5 (hc) -- ISBN 978-1-4109-3120-7 (pb) 1. United States--History--1919-1933--Sources--Juvenile literature. 2. United States--Social life and customs--1918-1945--Sources--Juvenile literature. 3. Nineteen twenties--Sources--Juvenile literature. I. Title.
   E784.P75 2008
   973.91--dc22

Acknowledgments
The author and publisher are grateful to the following for permission to reproduced copyright material: ©The Art Archive **pp. 18, 19**; ©Corbis **pp. 7T** (Bettmann), **10** (James van der Zee), **12** (Underwood & Underwood), **17** (CinemaPhoto), **23** (Bettmann), **26** (Bettmann), **27T**; ©Getty Images **pp. 9** (John Kobal Foundation), **13, 15, 24** (Hulton Archive), **20L** (Transcendental Graphics/Mark Rucker), **22** (Topical Press Agency); ©The Granger Collection **pp. 11** (New York/Rue des Archives), **25**; Library of Congress Prints and Photographs Division **pp. 4T, 4B, 5, 6, 7B, 8, 14, 20R, 21, 27B, 28, 29.**

Cover image of Congressman T.S. McMillan of South Carolina dancing the Charleston with Sylvia Clavans and Ruth Bennett, with Capitol building in the background, 1926, used with permission of ©Library of Congress Prints and Photographs Division.

The publishers would like to thank Nancy Harris for her assistance in the preparation of this book.

Contents

Some words are printed in bold, **like this**. You can find out what they mean on page 30.
You can also look in the box at the bottom of the page where they first appear.

Life in the 1920s

New machines made life easier. For instance, more people could buy cars than ever before. This led the country to build roads. These roads often led people to build **suburbs**. Suburbs are places to live just outside of cities. In the suburbs, people could buy a house for the first time. People also enjoyed many new things. There were new dances. There was a new type of music called jazz. For many people, it was a fun time. People called the 1920s the "Roaring Twenties."

Inventions like cars made life faster and louder.

But "roaring" was also a way to describe a really good time.

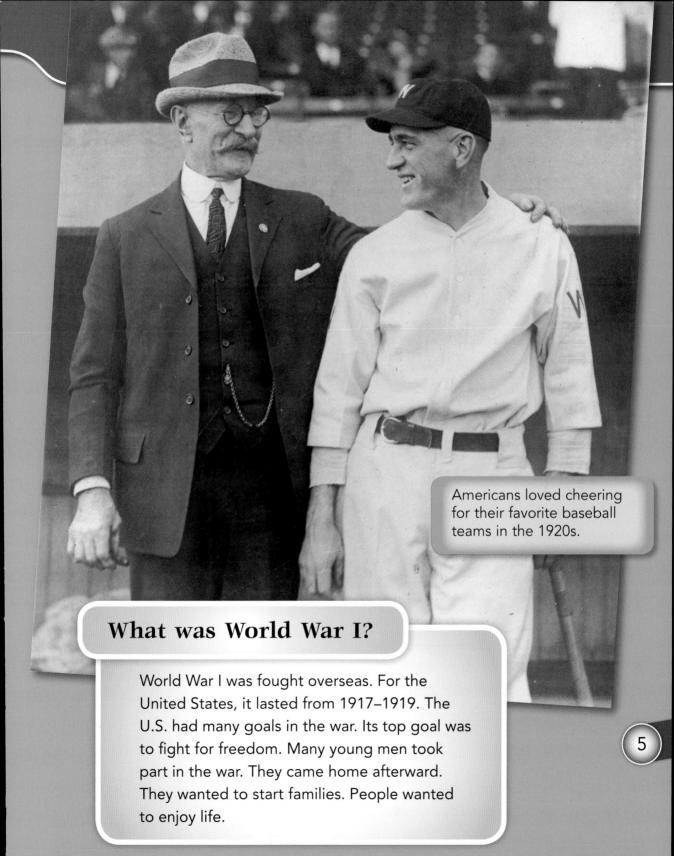

Americans loved cheering for their favorite baseball teams in the 1920s.

What was World War I?

World War I was fought overseas. For the United States, it lasted from 1917–1919. The U.S. had many goals in the war. Its top goal was to fight for freedom. Many young men took part in the war. They came home afterward. They wanted to start families. People wanted to enjoy life.

Not a drop to drink

The U.S. government makes the **laws** (rules). In 1920, the government made rules to get rid of alcohol. It became a crime to sell liquor. That included things like wine and beer. This was called **Prohibition**.

These policemen are dumping out liquor after a raid. This happened during Prohibition.

Al Capone

Bootleggers sold illegal liquor. They were criminals. Al Capone was the most famous bootlegger. He lived in the city of Chicago. Capone became rich. In secret, he paid police. He paid them to ignore his criminal acts. It took many years to put Capone in prison.

law	rule
Prohibition	period in the 1920s when liquor was illegal
bootlegger	criminal who sells illegal liquor

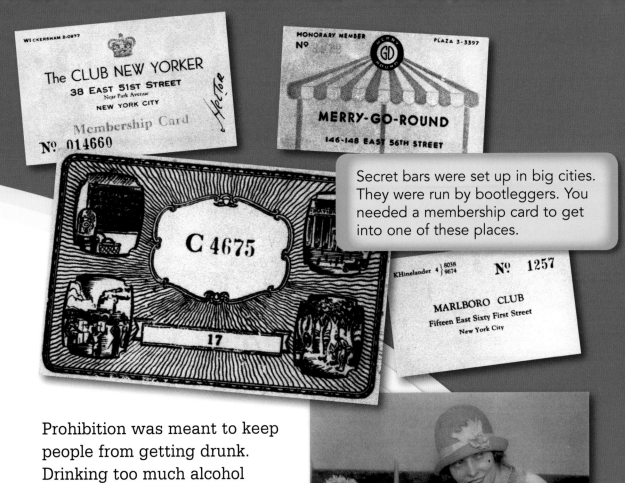

The CLUB NEW YORKER
38 EAST 51ST STREET
Near Park Avenue
NEW YORK CITY
WICKERSHAM 2-0977
Membership Card
№ 014660

HONORARY MEMBER
№
MERRY-GO-ROUND
146-148 EAST 56TH STREET
PLAZA 3-3397

C 4675
17

KHinelander 4 {8038 9674   № 1257
MARLBORO CLUB
Fifteen East Sixty First Street
New York City

Secret bars were set up in big cities. They were run by bootleggers. You needed a membership card to get into one of these places.

Prohibition was meant to keep people from getting drunk. Drinking too much alcohol causes health problems. Many people become hooked on alcohol. They cannot stop drinking it. Many others drink at bad times. They drink at work. They drink while driving.

But most adults disliked Prohibition. They wanted to drink alcohol sometimes. So they bought illegal liquor. They did this even though it was against the law. In 1933, the government stopped forbidding liquor. It could not make people quit. Prohibition was over.

This dancer shows off her hidden flask. It held illegal liquor.

Flappers

The Roaring Twenties were a time of change for women. They had more freedom than ever before.

In the past, young women were expected to get married quickly. Most were very young on their wedding day. Few women went to college. That began to change in the 1920s. More and more young women went to school. More worked outside the home. Some put off getting married as well.

This magazine cover shows a flapper dancing. Flappers wore short dresses to make dancing easier.

Many women **rebelled**. They refused to do what was expected. In the past, women wore long hair. They wore long dresses. That changed in the 1920s. Young women had their hair **bobbed**. That means it was cut short. They wore short dresses, jewelry, and makeup. They danced wild new dances.

Women who did this were called **flappers**. Flappers angered many older people. They did not want women to change.

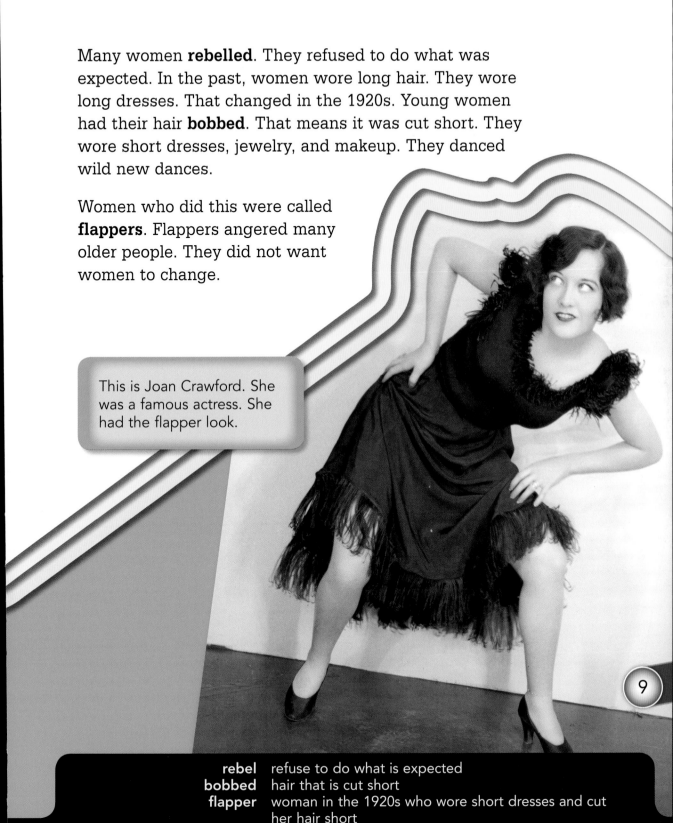

This is Joan Crawford. She was a famous actress. She had the flapper look.

9

rebel   refuse to do what is expected
bobbed   hair that is cut short
flapper   woman in the 1920s who wore short dresses and cut her hair short

Rebirth in Harlem

Life changed a lot for black Americans. Many blacks had lived in the South. But blacks in the South faced problems. White people there did not see them as equals. They did not allow blacks to vote for leaders of the country. That gave them no power in the government. Blacks also could not get good jobs. Blacks in the South were very poor.

In the early 1900s, many blacks moved north. They moved to big cities. In New York City, they moved to an area called Harlem. In the 1920s, Harlem was called "the capital of **Negro** America." (Negro was the word people used for blacks.) Harlem had many rich businessmen. It also had writers and artists. Harlem's musicians and dancers were well known.

Harlem attracted actors and dancers. It attracted artists and writers, too. Some black Americans became rich in Harlem.

Negro   word people used for a black American in the 1920s

Harlem had many dance halls. Whites and blacks both liked to visit them.

These people showed that black Americans could be special. Blacks were just as good as whites. The 1920s became known as the Harlem **Renaissance**. That means "rebirth" or "new start." It was a rebirth of respect for black people.

All That Jazz

Jazz music was born in the early 1900s. It was first played in the city of New Orleans. But it quickly spread. By the 1920s, young people everywhere loved jazz. It was louder than older types of music. It also allowed people to dance faster.

The Cotton Club was one of the most famous jazz clubs in Harlem.

Jazz songs were put onto records. The records were played on record players. Few people had record players before the 1920s. Records helped spread jazz music quickly. So did radios. Radios were new as well. Also, people could travel faster than ever before in the 1920s. Cars and airplanes were new to most people. That helped spread jazz music as well.

People heard jazz at dance halls. Young people danced for hours. There were many jazz musicians. One of the most famous was Louis Armstrong. He played the trumpet. Other well-known jazz players included Count Basie and Duke Ellington. People loved their songs. The 1920s are often called the Jazz Age.

Louis Armstrong was one of the very first people to play jazz. People still listen to his music today.

The Charleston

People loved to dance in the 1920s. It was one of the main ways of having fun. People danced at parties. Teenagers liked to dance at home. Schools even taught dancing.

The Charleston was a fast and fun dance!

People loved dancing the Charleston to the new **jazz** music.

The Charleston was a dance step. It became the biggest dance step of the 1920s. The Charleston was named after a city in the state of South Carolina. Young people liked the Charleston a lot. It let them swing their arms and legs. It allowed them to kick their feet. People could dance the Charleston with someone or they could dance it alone. Dancing the Charleston was exciting.

People liked other dances as well. They gave dances colorful names. One was called the foxtrot. Another was called the camel-walk. People also liked square dancing. In square dancing, they danced to country music. A "caller" told them what steps to make. The dancers had to keep up.

The Charleston   famous dance in the 1920s

Silent movies

Movies were silent during most of the 1920s. That means they had no sound. People did not know how to put sound with pictures. Instead, music played in the background.

The movies were also black-and-white. People did not know how to make color pictures yet.

Actors showed feelings in silent movies. But they had to use body movements. They had to use face movements. These took the place of words. Sometimes, actors "talked." The actor's lips would move. Then his words would appear printed on the screen. That would let people know what he said.

One of the biggest stars was Rudolph Valentino. Women loved Valentino. He was handsome and he always played the hero. Men liked Joan Crawford and Clara Bow. They often played **flappers** in movies.

Movies changed a lot in the 1920s. In 1927, the movie "The Jazz Singer" became the first to use sound. People called movies with sound "**talkies**." Talkies soon replaced silent movies.

talkie   movie with sound

This poster is for a Rudolph Valentino movie. He was a very popular actor in silent movies.

On the air

In 1920, the United States had just one radio station. It was in the city of Pittsburgh, Pennsylvania. That station played music. It gave people news. People liked listening to the radio. So more and more people set up radio stations. Also, more and more people bought radios. By the end of the 1920s, there were more than 600 radio stations. They were spread all over the country.

Where were the TVs?

There were no televisions in the early 1920s. The first working TV was not invented until 1927. Even then, it took many years for TV to catch on. Most Americans did not own TVs until the 1950s.

Radios became a common site in American living rooms.

Radio sets became common in homes. People put them in their living rooms. Radio changed family life. Before radio, people used to sit around and talk a lot. They read a lot and played games. Often they sang music. In the 1920s, families could also gather around their radio sets and listen.

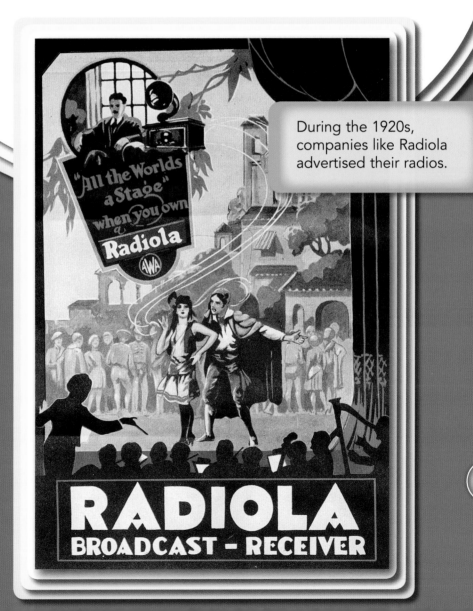

During the 1920s, companies like Radiola advertised their radios.

Good Sports

Americans loved sports in the 1920s. Baseball was America's No. 1 sport. The biggest star in baseball was Babe Ruth.

Ruth played for the New York Yankees. Ruth was a great hitter. He was best at hitting home runs. Ruth set records for hitting the most home runs. He hit the most home runs in one season. Ruth hit 60 homers in 1927. He set other records as well. It took many years for others to break those records. Ruth was very popular with kids. They liked to ask him for his **autograph** (signature).

Babe Ruth was the most popular sports star in the 1920s.

Red Grange became a star running back in college and in pro football.

Red Grange and Knute Rockne

People also loved college football. Red Grange was the biggest star. He played for the University of Illinois. He could run very fast. His nickname was the "Galloping Ghost." The biggest coach was Knute Rockne (*noot ROCK-nee*). He coached at Notre Dame University in Indiana. His teams did very well. Between 1918 and 1931, they won 105 games. They only lost 12.

Women make the sports page

In the early 1900s, most women were not allowed to play in sports. Ladies were not supposed to be good at sports. That idea changed a lot in the 1920s.

In 1926, Gertrude Ederle swam the English Channel. It is a body of water that is 21 miles wide. The Channel's waves are very big. Swimming it is tough. Gertrude was 19-years-old. She was the first woman to swim the Channel. It took Ederle 14 hours and 31 minutes. That was two hours faster than the men's record.

This picture shows Gertrude Ederle training for her swim across the English Channel.

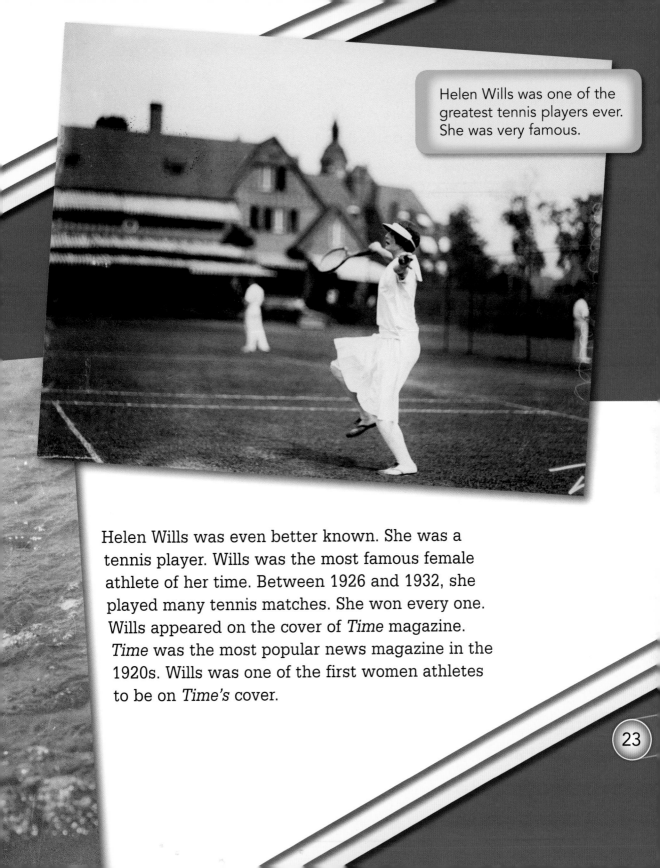

Helen Wills was one of the greatest tennis players ever. She was very famous.

Helen Wills was even better known. She was a tennis player. Wills was the most famous female athlete of her time. Between 1926 and 1932, she played many tennis matches. She won every one. Wills appeared on the cover of *Time* magazine. *Time* was the most popular news magazine in the 1920s. Wills was one of the first women athletes to be on *Time's* cover.

In the News

Airplanes were still new in the 1920s. Many people had never seen one. Some pilots flew around the country. They put on air shows. Their planes did tricks in the air. Sometimes pilots walked on the wings. They did it while the plane was in the air!

Many pilots tried to set new records. In 1927, Charles Lindbergh became one of them. He flew across the Atlantic Ocean alone. He was the first person to do so. It was a very brave thing to do. Lindbergh's airplane was small. It could have crashed. He might have been lost at sea.

Charles Lindbergh flew alone across the Atlantic Ocean. People called him "the Lone Eagle" and "Lucky Lindy."

24

Lindbergh's flight took 33 1/2 hours. He had to stay awake that whole time. Lindbergh became a hero overnight. People all over the world knew his name. Cities threw parades. Americans wanted to see him. Newspaper's called him "Lucky Lindy." That is because he was lucky to have survived.

LINDBERGH'S TOUR

When Colonel Lindbergh arrived in St. Louis, on February 13, he had flown about 9,060 miles, according to the following tabulation of the New York *Times*:

Date	Arrived at	Distance in Miles
Dec. 14	Mexico City	2,000
28	Guatemala City	675
30	British Honduras	280
Jan. 1	San Salvador	260
3	Honduras	180
5	Nicaragua	160
7	Costa Rica	280
9	Panama City	400
12	Colon	40
26	Colombia	400
27	Bogota, Colombia	425
29	Venezuela	650
31	Virgin Islands	1,000
Feb. 2	Porto Rico	80
4	Santo Domingo	250
6	Haiti	180
8	Cuba	600
13	St. Louis	1,200
	Total	9,060

SAN DIEGO to NEW YORK

NEW YORK to PARIS

GOOD WILL FLIGHT in UNITED STATES

PAN-AMERICAN FLIGHT

MILES
50 150 250 400
5 100 200 300 500

FORTY THOUSAND MILES THROUGH THE AIR

In a single year. This is the unblemished record of Col. Charles A. Lindbergh, who returned to St. Louis from his tour of Central America on February 13. During that time, he was in the air a total of 468 hours.

This map shows a long trip Lindbergh flew. There were lots of stops because everyone wanted to see him!

Crazy fads

The 1920s saw crazy **fads**. A fad is something that is popular for a brief time. Then it becomes less popular. For a while, young people had to have yo-yos. Then they lost interest in yo-yos. The same happened with roller skates.

Many fads were strange. These were two of the strangest.

Flag-pole sitting

This fad started in 1924. The first flagpole sitter was a man named "Shipwreck" Kelly. He sat on a small board. The board was on top of a tall pole. A flag-pole sitter had to sit very still. He had to keep from falling off or he might get hurt! Flagpole sitters stayed in place for hours.

Here's "Shipwreck" Kelly trying to set a new record!

Dance Marathons

Young people like to dance. Some tried to dance as long as they could. They danced in dance **marathons**. A marathon is a very long race. Some people hurt themselves at these marathons. Others made themselves sick. In one case, two people danced until they died.

Dance marathons like these were very hard. People had to have a lot of energy to make it to the end!

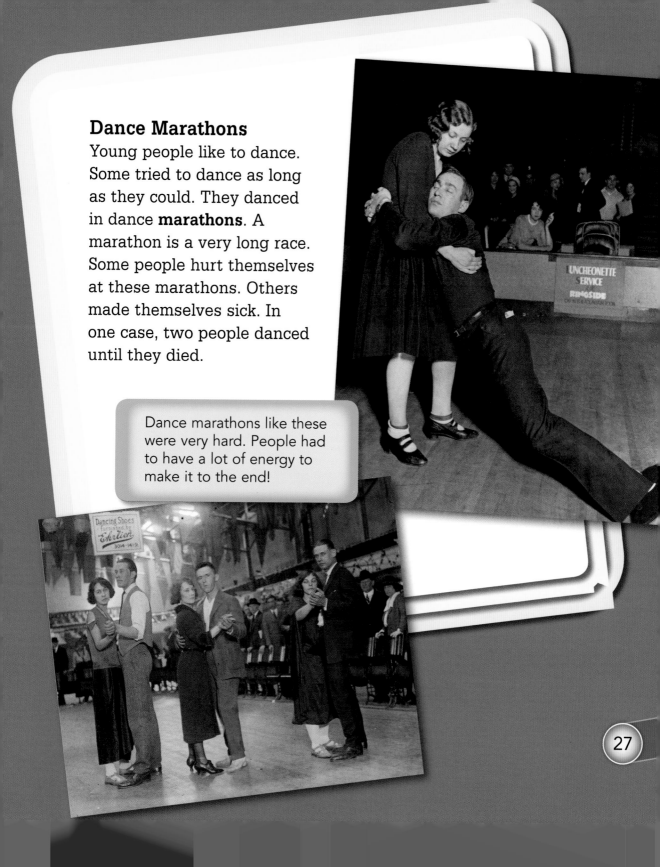

End of the Fun

In the 1920s, many people tried to get rich quick. A lot tried to make money on the **stock market**. The stock market is a place to buy and sell things. People there buy and sell shares of **stock**. Buying a share of stock makes someone a part-owner of a company. If the company does well, the share of stock costs more. If the company does poorly, the stock price goes down.

When the stock market crashed, many people lost all of their money.

stock something that gives a buyer part-ownership in a company

Crowds of people gathered right after the stock market crashed. They didn't know what to do!

In October 1929, prices for many stocks fell quickly. The stock market had crashed. People who had bought stock lost lots of money. That caused other bad things to happen. Many banks had bought stock. So those banks closed. Suddenly, people could not get their money out of the bank. Neither could companies. That caused factories to close. Stores closed. Many people could not find jobs.

These people became worried. They became scared. They did not feel like having fun. The Roaring Twenties were over. The 1930s would be a much harder time.

Glossary

autograph signature

bobbed cut short

bootlegger criminal who sells illegal liquor

The Charleston famous dance in the 1920s

fad something that is popular for a brief time and then becomes less popular

flapper woman in the 1920s who wore short dresses and cut her hair short

jazz type of music created in the early 1900s

law rule

marathon very long race

Negro word people used for a black American in the 1920s

Prohibition period in the 1920s when liquor was illegal

rebel refuse to do what is expected

renaissance rebirth or a fresh start

stock small amount of a company that someone can buy

stock market place to sell stocks

suburb place to live that is just outside a city

talkie movie with sound

Want to Know More?

Books to read

David Pietrusza. *The Roaring Twenties*. Chicago: Lucent Books, 1998.

Price, Sean. *Rebirth of a People: Harlem Renaissance*. Chicago: Raintree, 2006.

Websites

http://www.pbs.org/wgbh/amex/lindbergh/index.html
Visit this PBS website about Charles Lindbergh's incredible journey over the Atlantic.

http://www.baberuth.com/flash/about/biograph.html
Babe Ruth's official website explains his life and career.

http://www.pbs.org/jazz/
This website helps explain why the 1920s were called the Jazz Age.

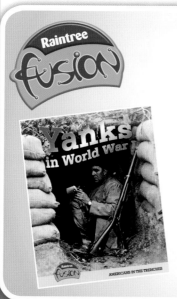

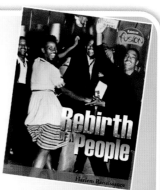

Read **Rebirth of a People: Harlem Renaissance** to find out about the interesting people and exciting places of Harlem's "Golden Age."

Read **Yanks in World War I: Americans in the Trenches** to find out about America's role in WWI.

Index